DATE DUE

H6S			

THE TRAIN OF STATES

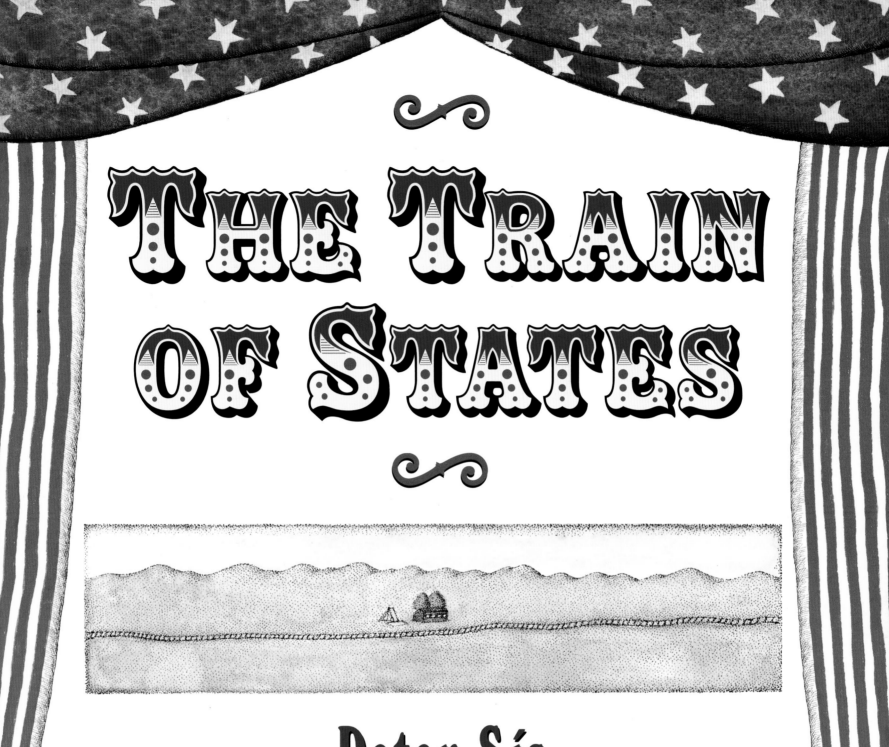

Peter Sís

GREENWILLOW BOOKS

An Imprint of HarperCollinsPublishers

The Train of States
Copyright © 2004 by Peter Sís
All rights reserved. Printed in the United States.
www.harperchildrens.com

Black line and watercolors
were used to prepare the full-color art.
The text type is Engraver Oldstyle.

Library of Congress Cataloging-in-Publication Data
Sís, Peter.
The train of states / by Peter Sís.
   p.   cm.
"Greenwillow Books."
Summary: Gives information about each state, including capital,
motto, state tree, state bird, source of name, and date of statehood.
ISBN 0-06-057838-6 (trade). ISBN 0-06-057839-4 (lib. bdg.)
1. U.S. states—Miscellanea—Juvenile literature. 2. United
States—Miscellanea—Juvenile literature. [1. U.S. states—
Miscellanea. 2. United States—Miscellanea.] I. Title.
E180.S58 2004 973'.02—dc22 2003056826
10 9 8 7 6 5 4 3 2 1
First Edition

Greenwillow Books

*To twenty-two years in the United States
and twenty years with Greenwillow Books*

The Train of States is a personal journey that combines my love for my adopted country with my admiration for antique circus wagons. There are hundreds of facts, symbols, moments from history, tidbits, and details presented on these pages—many of them open to interpretation; several of them the topic of ongoing debate. I hope my book will lead you on your own journeys of discovery.

Very special thanks to Martha Mihalick and Anne Dunn, fact-checkers extraordinaire, and to Virginia Bartow of the Humanities and Social Sciences Library, The New York Public Library, for their relentless investigation of the materials presented in this book.

—Peter Sís

"LIBERTY AND INDEPENDENCE"

PEACH BLOSSOM

AMERICAN HOLLY

SWEET GOLDENROD

LADYBUG

WEAKFISH

TIGER SWALLOWTAIL

BLUE HEN CHICKEN

FIRST STATE

DATE OF STATEHOOD

1. DELAWARE December 7, 1787

Named for Baron de la Warr, English governor of Virginia

Dover

American holly

peach blossom

blue hen chicken

In 1880, the first beauty contest in the U.S. was held in Rehoboth Beach. Thomas Edison was one of the three judges.

BENJAMIN FRANKLIN

HEMLOCK

HERSHEY'S KISS

RUFFED GROUSE

TRILOBITE

MOUNTAIN LAUREL

KEYSTONE STATE

GREAT DANE

BROOK TROUT

BETSY ROSS

MARIAN ANDERSON

JAMES BUCHANAN

FIRST LIBRARY

"VIRTUE, LIBERTY, AND INDEPENDENCE"

DATE OF STATEHOOD

2. PENNSYLVANIA December 12, 1787

Named for Adm. Sir William Penn and the Latin *silva*, meaning "woodland"

Harrisburg

hemlock

mountain laurel

ruffed grouse

When legislators made the Great Dane the state dog in 1965, they voted with yips, growls, and barks.

GARDEN STATE

VIOLET

GROVER CLEVELAND

HONEYBEE

THOMAS EDISON

RED OAK

EASTERN GOLDFINCH

BROOK TROUT

"LIBERTY AND PROSPERITY"

DATE OF STATEHOOD

3. NEW JERSEY December 18, 1787

Named for the Channel Isle of Jersey in England

Trenton

red oak

violet

eastern goldfinch

The "Bone Wars"—a bitter feud between paleontologists—began in New Jersey ten years after the first nearly complete dinosaur skeleton was found there in 1858.

SHARK TOOTH

CHEROKEE ROSE

PEACH STATE

JIMMY CARTER

BROWN THRASHER

TIGER SWALLOWTAIL

LARGEMOUTH BASS

LIVE OAK

RIGHT WHALE

"WISDOM, JUSTICE, AND MODERATION"

DATE OF STATEHOOD

4. GEORGIA January 2, 1788

Named for England's King George II

⭐ Atlanta

🌳 live oak

🌱 Cherokee rose

🐦 brown thrasher

Civil rights activist and Atlanta native Martin Luther King, Jr., was born Michael Luther King; he was renamed when he was six.

CONSTITUTION STATE

AMERICAN ROBIN

MOUNTAIN LAUREL

YANKEE DOODLE

P. T. BARNUM

WHITE OAK

OYSTERS

GEORGE W. BUSH

"HE WHO TRANSPLANTED STILL SUSTAINS"

DATE OF STATEHOOD

5. CONNECTICUT January 9, 1788

Named for the Mohegan Indian *quinnehtukqut*, meaning "beside the long tidal river."

Hartford

white oak

The first hamburger was served in 1895 at Louie's Lunch in New Haven.

mountain laurel

American robin

MASSASOIT
TURKEY
BLACK-CAPPED CHICKADEE

BAY STATE

JOHN ADAMS
JOHN QUINCY ADAMS
PHILLIS WHEATLEY
LOUISA MAY ALCOTT
JOHN F. KENNEDY
GEORGE H. W. BUSH

PAUL REVERE
AMERICAN ELM
MAYFLOWER
NEPTUNE SHELL
LADYBUG
ALEXANDER GRAHAM BELL
NORTHERN RIGHT WHALE
CAPE COD
COD

BOSTON TERRIER
MORGAN HORSE

"BY THE SWORD WE SEEK PEACE, BUT PEACE ONLY UNDER LIBERTY"

DATE OF STATEHOOD

6. MASSACHUSETTS February 6, 1788

Named for the Algonquian Indian word meaning "at the big hill"

 Boston

 mayflower

American elm

black-capped chickadee

 In 1891, James Naismith invented the game of basketball in Springfield. The first game was played with a soccer ball and peach baskets hung ten feet in the air.

FIRST REFRIGERATOR

BALTIMORE CHECKERSPOT

HARRIET TUBMAN

KING WILLIAM'S SCHOOL

STRIPED BASS

WHITE OAK

DIAMONDBACK TERRAPIN

BLACK-EYED SUSAN

BALTIMORE ORIOLE

OLD LINE STATE

CALICO CAT

CHESAPEAKE BAY RETRIEVER

"MANLY DEEDS, WOMANLY WORDS"

DATE OF STATEHOOD

7. MARYLAND April 28, 1788

Named for Henrietta Maria, queen to England's Charles I

★ Annapolis

white oak

Francis Scott Key wrote "The Star-Spangled Banner" from a British ship in the Baltimore harbor in 1814.

black-eyed Susan

Baltimore oriole

PALMETTO STATE

ANDREW JACKSON

BLUE GRANITE

PEACH

EASTERN TIGER SWALLOWTAIL

YELLOW JESSAMINE

SPOTTED SALAMANDER

CAROLINA WREN

BOYKIN SPANIEL

"PREPARED IN MIND AND RESOURCES"
"WHILE I BREATHE, I HOPE"

8. SOUTH CAROLINA
May 23, 1788

DATE OF STATEHOOD

Named for England's King Charles I

Columbia

palmetto

yellow jessamine

Carolina wren

South Carolina is considered to have some of the most pristine nesting areas for loggerhead sea turtles, a threatened species.

BERYL

CORNISH-WINDSOR BRIDGE

GRANITE

GRANITE STATE

FRANKLIN PIERCE

PURPLE LILAC

PINK LADY'S SLIPPER

FIRST FREE LIBRARY

PURPLE FINCH

WHITE BIRCH

"LIVE FREE OR DIE"

STRIPED BASS

KARNER BLUE

BROOK TROUT

DATE OF STATEHOOD

9. NEW HAMPSHIRE June 21, 1788

Named for Hampshire County, England

Concord

white birch

purple lilac

purple finch

The Brattle Organ in Portsmouth's St. John's Church is the oldest pipe organ in the United States. Still played on special occasions, it dates back to 1708.

GEORGE WASHINGTON • THOMAS JEFFERSON • JAMES MADISON • JAMES MONROE • WILLIAM HENRY HARRISON • JOHN TYLER • ZACHARY TAYLOR • WOODROW WILSON

CARDINAL

BROOK TROUT

"THUS ALWAYS TO TYRANTS"

MOUNT VERNON

MONTICELLO

TIGER SWALLOWTAIL

DOGWOOD

POCAHONTAS

OLD DOMINION STATE

10. VIRGINIA
DATE OF STATEHOOD
June 25, 1788
Named for England's Queen Elizabeth I, the Virgin Queen

 Richmond

dogwood

 dogwood

cardinal

Both the Revolutionary War and the Civil War ended in Virginia, the first in Yorktown in 1781 and the second at Appomattox Court House in 1865.

EMPIRE STATE

FRANKLIN D. ROOSEVELT

THEODORE ROOSEVELT

SUSAN B. ANTHONY

ROSE
BROOK TROUT
PRETZEL

BLUEBIRD
SUGAR MAPLE

MARTIN VAN BUREN

MILLARD FILLMORE

"EVER   UPWARD"

SOJOURNER TRUTH

ELEANOR ROOSEVELT

DATE OF STATEHOOD

11. NEW YORK July 26, 1788

Named for England's Duke of York

 Albany

 sugar maple

 rose

 bluebird

Chittenango, birthplace of *The Wizard of Oz* author L. Frank Baum, has a yellow brick road and an annual Munchkin parade.

ANDREW JOHNSON

JAMES POLK

GREAT SMOKY MOUNTAINS

BLUEBERRY   CARDINAL   DOGWOOD   CHANNEL BASS   PINE   PLOTT HOUND

TAR HEEL STATE

FIRST GOLD NUGGET

EASTERN BOX TURTLE

"TO BE RATHER THAN TO SEEM"

DATE OF STATEHOOD

12. NORTH CAROLINA
November 21, 1789

Named for England's King Charles I

Raleigh

pine

dogwood

cardinal

The Roanoke Island colony vanished between 1587, when leader John White went back to England for supplies, and 1590, when he returned. The only clue was the word "Croatoan" carved into a tree.

RED MAPLE

GREENING APPLE

RHODE ISLAND RED

VIOLET

STRIPED BASS

OCEAN STATE

OLDEST SCHOOLHOUSE

OLDEST CAROUSEL

FIRST CIRCUS

"HOPE"

DATE OF STATEHOOD

13. RHODE ISLAND May 29, 1790

Named for the Greek island of Rhodes

⭐ **Providence**

🌳 **red maple**

The Flying Horse Carousel in Watch Hill is the oldest carousel in the U.S. in continuous operation.

🌸 **violet**

🐦 **Rhode Island red**

CHESTER ARTHUR

CALVIN COOLIDGE

"FREEDOM   AND UNITY"

WALLEYE PIKE

BROOK TROUT

HERMIT
THRUSH

MONARCH

HONEYBEE

SUGAR   MAPLE

MORGAN
HORSE

RED
CLOVER

NORTHERN
LEOPARD
FROG

MAPLE
SYRUP

GREEN MOUNTAIN STATE

DATE OF STATEHOOD

14. VERMONT March 4, 1791

Named for the French words *vert mont*, meaning "green mountain"

 Montpelier

sugar maple

 Vermont's was the first
state constitution to
outlaw slavery—in 1777.

 red clover

 hermit thrush

BLUEGRASS STATE

BLUEGRASS MUSIC

ABRAHAM LINCOLN

CARDINAL

KENTUCKY BASS

VICEROY

BEAGLE

GRAY SQUIRREL

GOLDENROD

TULIP TREE

MAMMOTH CAVE

"UNITED WE STAND, DIVIDED WE FALL"

15. KENTUCKY

DATE OF STATEHOOD
June 1, 1792

Named for the Iroquois Indian word meaning "land of tomorrow"

 Frankfort

 tulip tree

 goldenrod

 cardinal

More than six billion dollars' worth of gold is held in the underground vaults of Fort Knox. This is the largest amount of gold stored anywhere in the world.

ELVIS PRESLEY

CHANNEL CATFISH

MOCKINGBIRD

VOLUNTEER STATE

ZEBRA SWALLOWTAIL

FIRST U. S. GUIDE DOG

BOX TURTLE

LIGHTNING BUG

LARGEMOUTH BASS

TULIP TREE

IRIS

RACCOON

"AGRICULTURE AND COMMERCE"

16. TENNESSEE June 1, 1796

DATE OF STATEHOOD

Named for *Tanasi,* an important Cherokee Indian village

 Nashville

 tulip tree

 iris

 mockingbird

 Morris Frank from Nashville was the first American to use a guide dog for the blind. His dog, Buddy, was a female German shepherd he brought home from a guide dog school in Switzerland.

BUCKEYE STATE

RUTHERFORD B. HAYES

JAMES GARFIELD

BENJAMIN HARRISON

WILLIAM MCKINLEY

WILLIAM H. TAFT

WARREN HARDING

ULYSSES S. GRANT

CARDINAL

FIRST CHEWING GUM PATENT

FIRST HOT DOG

NEIL ARMSTRONG

TECUMSEH

ANNIE OAKLEY

SCARLET CARNATION

JOHN GLENN

BLACK RACER

TRILOBITE

FIRST PROFESSIONAL BASEBALL TEAM

BUCKEYE

"WITH GOD ALL THINGS ARE POSSIBLE"

DATE OF STATEHOOD

17. OHIO March 1, 1803

Named for the Iroquois Indian word *oheo*, meaning "great river"

 Columbus

 buckeye

In 1879, Cleveland became the first city in the U.S. to have electric street lamps.

 scarlet carnation

cardinal

PELICAN STATE

BALD CYPRESS · CATAHOULA LEOPARD DOG · MAGNOLIA · IRIS · BLACK BEAR · MELODEON

NEW ORLEANS

BROWN PELICAN

ALLIGATOR

"UNION, JUSTICE, AND CONFIDENCE"

DATE OF STATEHOOD

18. LOUISIANA April 30, 1812

Named for King Louis XIV of France

Baton Rouge

bald cypress

magnolia

brown pelican

The town of Jean Lafitte is named after the legendary buccaneer and veteran of the Battle of New Orleans and War of 1812.

HOOSIER STATE

FIRST AIRMAIL

CARDINAL

PEONY

LITTLE 500

JOHNNY APPLESEED

TULIP TREE

"THE CROSSROADS OF AMERICA"

DATE OF STATEHOOD

19. INDIANA December 11, 1816

Name created by settlers, meaning "land of the Indians"

Indianapolis   tulip tree

peony   cardinal

So many slaves were sheltered in Levi Coffin's Fountain City home that it was known as the "Grand Central Station" of the Underground Railroad.

PUSHMATAHA

HONEYBEE

SPICEBUSH
SWALLOWTAIL

MAGNOLIA STATE

MAGNOLIA

WOOD DUCK

THE
BLUES

MOCKINGBIRD

LARGEMOUTH BASS

"BY VALOR AND ARMS"

DATE OF STATEHOOD

20. MISSISSIPPI December 10, 1817

Named for the Chippewa Indian words *mici zibi*, meaning "great river"

Jackson

magnolia

magnolia

mockingbird

On May 11, 1887, a
6 x 8 inch gopher turtle
completely encased in ice
fell from the sky during
a severe hailstorm near
Bovina.

RONALD REAGAN

ILLINOIS

MONARCH

PRAIRIE STATE

WHITE OAK

BLUEGILL

"STATE SOVEREIGNTY, NATIONAL UNION"

CHICAGO

CARDINAL

WHITE-TAILED DEER

ABRAHAM LINCOLN

VIOLET

DATE OF STATEHOOD

21. ILLINOIS December 3, 1818

Named for a French corruption of the Algonquian Indian word meaning "superior men"

 Springfield

white oak

 violet

 cardinal

 The Home Insurance Building in Chicago was the world's first modern skyscraper. It was 138 feet high.

HELEN KELLER

ROSA PARKS

HEART OF DIXIE

CAMELLIA

LARGEMOUTH BASS

FIGHTING TARPON

RED-BELLIED TURTLE

SOUTHERN LONGLEAF PINE

RACKING HORSE

MONARCH

YELLOWHAMMER

WILD TURKEY

"WE DARE DEFEND OUR RIGHTS"

DATE OF STATEHOOD

22. ALABAMA December 14, 1819

Name may be from the Alibamu Indians, members of the Creek Confederacy.
Possibly from the Choctaw language, *alba ayamule*, meaning "I clear the thicket."

Montgomery

southern longleaf pine

camellia

yellowhammer

Rosa Parks refused to give up her seat on a city bus in 1955, which began the Montgomery bus boycott.

PINE TREE
STATE

HONEYBEE

CHICKADEE

WINTERGREEN

MAINE COON CAT

WHITE PINE CONE
& TASSEL

WILD
BLUEBERRY

LANDLOCKED
SALMON

"I LEAD"

DATE OF STATEHOOD

23. MAINE March 15, 1820

Name may have originated from explorers referring to the "mainland," from a province
in northwestern France, or from a town on the coast of England

 Augusta

 white pine

 white pine cone
and tassel

chickadee

Margaret Chase Smith of
Skowhegan became the
first woman to serve in
both houses of Congress
when she was elected to
the Senate in 1948.

SHOW-ME STATE

PONY EXPRESS

FIRST ICE-CREAM CONES

SPIRIT OF ST. LOUIS

GATEWAY ARCH

BLUEBIRD

HONEYBEE

FLOWERING DOGWOOD

HARRY TRUMAN

SCOTT JOPLIN

MARK TWAIN

HAWTHORN

PADDLEFISH

CHANNEL CATFISH

"THE WELFARE OF THE PEOPLE
SHALL BE THE SUPREME LAW"

DATE OF STATEHOOD

24. MISSOURI August 10, 1821

Named for a Sioux Indian tribe; the word *missouri* means "town of the large canoes"

Jefferson City   flowering dogwood   Ice-cream cones were first served at the Louisiana Purchase Exposition of 1904, also known as the St. Louis World's Fair.

hawthorn   bluebird

NATURAL STATE

MOCKINGBIRD

WILLIAM J. CLINTON

SOUTH ARKANSAS VINE RIPE PINK TOMATO

HONEYBEE

PINE

APPLE BLOSSOM

WHITE-TAILED DEER

"THE PEOPLE RULE"

DATE OF STATEHOOD

25. ARKANSAS June 15, 1836

Named for the Quapaw Indians, who were called Akansea, meaning "south wind," by other tribes

Little Rock

pine

The World's Championship Duck Calling Contest is held annually in Stuttgart.

apple blossom

mockingbird

GREAT LAKE STATE

ANTOINE DE LA MOTHE CADILLAC

"IF YOU SEEK A PLEASANT PENINSULA, LOOK ABOUT YOU"

APPLE BLOSSOM

WHITE PINE

ROBIN

BROOK TROUT

DWARF LAKE IRIS

WHITE-TAILED DEER

PAINTED TURTLE

DATE OF STATEHOOD

26. MICHIGAN January 26, 1837

Named for the Algonquian Indian word *michigama*, meaning "great lake"

 Lansing

white pine

 apple blossom

 robin

In 1866 James Vernor of Detroit created his recipe for ginger ale, the first soft drink made in the U.S.

ORANGE BLOSSOM

MOCKINGBIRD

SUNSHINE STATE

KENNEDY SPACE CENTER

SABAL PALM

PONCE DE LEON'S EXPEDITION

LARGEMOUTH BASS

SAILFISH

HORSE CONCH

"IN GOD WE TRUST"

PANTHER

ALLIGATOR

DATE OF STATEHOOD

27. FLORIDA March 3, 1845

Named for Pascua Florida, the Spanish Eastertime "Feast of Flowers," by the explorer Ponce de Leon

⭐ Tallahassee

🌳 sabal palm

About one million alligators live in the state of Florida.

🌱 orange blossom

🐦 mockingbird

LONE STAR STATE

ARMADILLO

HORNED LIZARD

PRICKLY PEAR CACTUS

BLUEBONNET

MOCKINGBIRD

PECAN

DWIGHT D. EISENHOWER

LYNDON B. JOHNSON

GUADALUPE BASS

MONARCH

MEXICAN FREE-TAILED BAT

LIGHTNING WHELK

"FRIENDSHIP"

DATE OF STATEHOOD

28. TEXAS December 29, 1845

Named for the Caddo Indian word *tejas*, meaning "friends" or "allies"

Austin

pecan

bluebonnet

mockingbird

In 1856, Jefferson Davis had camels imported to transport military provisions across west Texas. The Camel Corps had mixed success and ended in 1861.

"OUR LIBERTIES WE PRIZE, AND OUR RIGHTS WE WILL MAINTAIN"

HERBERT HOOVER

GEODE

EASTERN GOLDFINCH

HAWKEYE STATE

OAK

WILD ROSE

ANTONÍN DVOŘÁK

IOWA

DATE OF STATEHOOD

29. IOWA December 28, 1846

Named for the Iowa Indians

Des Moines

oak

wild rose

eastern goldfinch

Every year since 1960, the Iowa State Fair has featured a 600-pound butter sculpture of a dairy cow.

BADGER STATE

WISCONSIN
1848

HARRY HOUDINI   FRANK LLOYD WRIGHT   AMERICAN WATER SPANIEL   GENERAL MACARTHUR

TRILOBITE   GREEN BAY PACKERS

ROBIN

DAIRY COW

HONEYBEE

SUGAR MAPLE   WOOD VIOLET

MUSKELLUNGE

"FORWARD"

30. WISCONSIN May 29, 1848

DATE OF STATEHOOD

Named for the French version of a Chippewa Indian term meaning "grassy place"

⭐ Madison

🌳 sugar maple

🌱 wood violet

🐦 robin

Every year the Great Circus Parade—a re-creation of the old-time street parades of wagons, animals, and performers—rolls through downtown Milwaukee.

CALIFORNIA REPUBLIC

JOAQUIN MURIETA

GOLD

GOLDEN TROUT

CESAR CHAVEZ

CALIFORNIA QUAIL

GARIBALDI

GOLDEN STATE

GRAY WHALE

GOLDEN POPPY

DOGFACE

DESERT TORTOISE

MOUNT WHITNEY

CALIFORNIA REDWOOD

RICHARD M. NIXON

MARTHA GRAHAM

"EUREKA"

DATE OF STATEHOOD

31. CALIFORNIA September 9, 1850

Named for an island paradise in a popular Spanish novel from around 1510

Sacramento

California redwood

golden poppy

California quail

The first blue jeans were created in 1853 by Levi Strauss and became the uniform for gold prospectors.

PINK AND WHITE LADY'S SLIPPER

RED PINE

NORTH STAR STATE

MOREL

MONARCH

WALLEYE

TWIN CITIES

COMMON LOON

"THE STAR OF THE NORTH"

32. MINNESOTA
May 11, 1858

Named for the Dakota Indian word meaning "sky-tinted water"

 St. Paul

red pine

 pink and white lady's slipper

common loon

The 130-feet-tall ice palace constructed for the 1888 St. Paul Winter Carnival was by far the city's tallest building at the time.

BEAVER STATE

"SHE FLIES WITH HER OWN WINGS"

WESTERN MEADOWLARK

OREGON GRAPE

DOUGLAS FIR

OREGON SWALLOWTAIL

HAZELNUT

CHINOOK SALMON

CHIEF JOSEPH

PACIFIC GOLDEN CHANTERELLE

STATE OF OREGON
1859

DATE OF STATEHOOD

33. OREGON February 14, 1859

The origins of "Oregon" are uncertain, but it was likely derived from an Indian word.

Salem

Douglas fir

Oregon grape

western meadowlark

Formed more than 7,000 years ago, Crater Lake is the deepest lake in the U.S., with an average depth of 1,500 feet and a maximum depth of 1,949 feet.

"TO THE STARS THROUGH DIFFICULTIES"

WESTERN MEADOWLARK

ORNATE BOX TURTLE

NATIVE SUNFLOWER

COTTONWOOD

BARRED TIGER SALAMANDER

CHANNEL CATFISH

HONEYBEE

KANSAS

SUNFLOWER STATE

DATE OF STATEHOOD

34. KANSAS January 29, 1861

Named for the Kansa Indians; *kansa* means "people of the south wind"

Topeka

cottonwood

The geographic center of the continental 48 United States is located in Smith County, near Lebanon, in north-central Kansas.

native sunflower

western meadowlark

GOLDEN DELICIOUS APPLE

MOUNTAIN STATE

THOMAS "STONEWALL" JACKSON

BROOK TROUT

CARDINAL

MONARCH

SUGAR MAPLE

HONEYBEE

RHODODENDRON

ORGAN CAVE

"MOUNTAINEERS ARE ALWAYS FREE"

DATE OF STATEHOOD

35. WEST VIRGINIA June 20, 1863

Named for England's Queen Elizabeth I, the Virgin Queen

Charleston

sugar maple

rhododendron

cardinal

The continent's largest conical burial mound is in Moundsville. It is 69 feet high and 295 feet in diameter.

SILVER STATE

MOUNTAIN BLUEBIRD

DESERT
TORTOISE

TURQUOISE

SINGLE-LEAF
PIÑON

LAHONTAN CUTTHROAT TROUT

DESERT BIGHORN SHEEP

SAGEBRUSH

BRISTLECONE
PINE

"ALL FOR OUR COUNTRY"

36. NEVADA October 31, 1864

Named for the Spanish word *nevada*, meaning "snow-capped"

 Carson City

single-leaf piñon and bristlecone pine

sagebrush

mountain bluebird

Hard hats were first invented in 1933 specifically for workers on the Hoover Dam, the largest single public works project of its day.

CORNHUSKER STATE

COTTONWOOD

WESTERN MEADOWLARK

WHITE-TAILED DEER

HONEYBEE

GERALD FORD

MAMMOTH

GOLDENROD

BLUE CHALCEDONY

CHANNEL CATFISH

"EQUALITY BEFORE THE LAW"

DATE OF STATEHOOD

37. NEBRASKA March 1, 1867

Named for the Oto Indian word *nebrathka*, meaning "flat water"

Lincoln

cottonwood

The longest porch swing in the world is in Hebron. It can seat eighteen adults or twenty-four children.

goldenrod

western meadowlark

CENTENNIAL STATE

"NOTHING WITHOUT THE DEITY"

BLUE GRAMA GRASS

BLUE SPRUCE

WHITE AND LAVENDER COLUMBINE

HAIRSTREAK

GREENBACK CUTTHROAT TROUT

LARK BUNTING

DATE OF STATEHOOD

38. COLORADO August 1, 1876

Named for the Spanish word *colorado*, meaning "red" or "ruddy"

Denver

blue spruce

white and lavender columbine

lark bunting

After gold was discovered near Pikes Peak in 1858, the slogan "Pikes Peak or Bust" began appearing painted on prairie schooners (the covered wagons used by pioneers).

PEACE GARDEN STATE

NORTHERN PIKE

AMERICAN ELM

NOKOTA

WESTERN MEADOWLARK

INTERNATIONAL PEACE GARDEN

WILD PRAIRIE ROSE

SACAGAWEA

THEODORE ROOSEVELT

"LIBERTY AND UNION, NOW AND FOREVER, ONE AND INSEPARABLE"

39. NORTH DAKOTA November 2, 1889

DATE OF STATEHOOD

Named for the Sioux Indian word *dakota*, meaning "friend"

Bismarck

American elm

wild prairie rose

western meadowlark

North Dakota has 63 National Wildlife Refuges, more than any other state.

MOUNT RUSHMORE STATE

KUCHEN

BLACK HILLS SPRUCE

PASQUEFLOWER

WALLEYE

WILD BILL HICKOCK

HONEYBEE

COYOTE

"UNDER GOD THE PEOPLE RULE"

DATE OF STATEHOOD

40. SOUTH DAKOTA November 2, 1889

Named for the Sioux Indian word *dakota*, meaning "friend"

Pierre

Black Hills spruce

pasqueflower

ring-necked pheasant

Sue, the largest and most intact *T. rex* fossil, was discovered by Sue Hendrickson in 1990 near the town of Faith.

BIG SKY COUNTRY

TREASURE STATE

MONTANA

"GOLD AND SILVER"

WESTERN MEADOWLARK

MOURNING CLOAK

PONDEROSA PINE

BITTERROOT

BLACKSPOTTED CUTTHROAT TROUT

DATE OF STATEHOOD

41. MONTANA November 8, 1889

Named for the Latin *montaanus*, meaning "mountainous"

Helena

Ponderosa pine

In Montana elk, deer, and antelope outnumber humans.

bitterroot

western meadowlark

STEELHEAD TROUT

EVERGREEN STATE

AMERICAN GOLDFINCH

APPLE

GREEN DARNER DRAGONFLY

PETRIFIED WOOD

"BY AND BY"

COAST RHODODENDRON

WESTERN HEMLOCK

42. WASHINGTON *November 11, 1889*

DATE OF STATEHOOD

Named for George Washington, the first U.S. president

 Olympia

western hemlock

 Coast rhododendron

 American goldfinch

In 1980, Mount St. Helens, a volcano in the Cascade Range that had been dormant since 1857, erupted in one of the biggest volcanic disturbances in U.S. history.

GEM STATE

MONARCH

IDAHO STAR GARNET

SYRINGA

HUCKLEBERRY

CUTTHROAT TROUT

MOUNTAIN BLUEBIRD

WESTERN WHITE PINE

"LET IT BE PERPETUAL"

DATE OF STATEHOOD

43. IDAHO July 3, 1890

Name was coined or invented, and was originally used for a Columbia River steamship

Boise

western white pine

The state capitol building in Boise is heated by underground hot springs.

syringa

mountain bluebird

OLD FAITHFUL

EQUALITY STATE

DEVILS TOWER

CUTTHROAT TROUT

WESTERN MEADOWLARK

INDIAN PAINTBRUSH

PLAINS COTTONWOOD

JADE

FIRST VOTE FOR WOMEN

"EQUAL RIGHTS"

DATE OF STATEHOOD

44. WYOMING July 10, 1890

Named for the Delaware Indian words meaning "at the big plains"

 Cheyenne plains cottonwood

Indian paintbrush

 western meadowlark

Thousands of people traveling west on the Oregon Trail scratched their names on the surface of Independence Rock, which sits fifty miles southwest of Casper.

INDIAN RICE GRASS

BEEHIVE STATE

SEGO LILY

CALIFORNIA GULL

BLUE SPRUCE

DUBHE

TOPAZ

CHERRY

BONNEVILLE

ROCKY MOUNTAIN ELK

CUTTHROAT TROUT

"INDUSTRY"

45. UTAH

DATE OF STATEHOOD

January 4, 1896

Named for the Ute Indians (people of the mountains)

Salt Lake City

blue spruce

sego lily

California gull

Great Salt Lake is the fourth largest terminal (no outlet) lake in the world, three to five times saltier than the ocean, and free of fish (the largest marine creatures are brine shrimp).

SOONER STATE

BULL FROG

COLLARED LIZARD

BLACK SWALLOWTAIL

MISTLETOE

INDIAN BLANKET

FIDDLE

WHITE BASS

REDBUD

SCISSOR-TAILED FLYCATCHER

OKLAHOMA

"LABOR CONQUERS ALL THINGS"

DATE OF STATEHOOD

46. OKLAHOMA November 16, 1907

Named for the Choctaw Indian words meaning "red people"

⭐ Oklahoma City

🌳 redbud

🌿 mistletoe

🐦 scissor-tailed flycatcher

Oklahoma has the only state capitol building in the world with an oil well drilled beneath it.

LAND OF ENCHANTMENT

GEORGIA O'KEEFFE

TARANTULA HAWK WASP

BLACK BEAR

"IT GROWS AS IT GOES"

PIÑON

CUTTHROAT TROUT

YUCCA

DATE OF STATEHOOD

47. NEW MEXICO January 6, 1912

Named by Spanish explorers, for Mexico

⭐ Santa Fe

piñon

yucca

roadrunner

The city of Santa Fe was settled in 1607, making it the oldest state capital city in the country.

GRAND CANYON STATE

CACTUS WREN

APACHE TROUT

SAGUARO CACTUS BLOSSOM

GRAND CANYON

PALO VERDE

ARIZONA TREE FROG

TWO-TAILED SWALLOWTAIL

ARIZONA RIDGENOSE RATTLESNAKE

GERONIMO

"GOD ENRICHES"

48. **ARIZONA** February 14, 1912

DATE OF STATEHOOD

Named for the Papago Indian word *arizonac*, meaning "place of the small spring"

Phoenix

blossom of the saguaro cactus

palo verde

cactus wren

In 1930, Clyde Tombaugh at Lowell Observatory in Flagstaff discovered the planet Pluto.

THE LAST FRONTIER

GOLD

MOOSE

BOWHEAD WHALE

FOUR-SPOT SKIMMER DRAGONFLY

SITKA SPRUCE

WILLOW PTARMIGAN

FORGET-ME-NOT

KING SALMON

"NORTH TO THE FUTURE"

DATE OF STATEHOOD

49. ALASKA January 3, 1959

Named for the Aleut word *alyeska*, meaning "great land"

 Juneau

Sitka spruce

 forget-me-not

 willow ptarmigan

 In Barrow, Alaska's northernmost point, the sun doesn't set for 84 days during the summer months.

NENE

KILAUEA

HALEAKALA

BLACK CORAL

QUEEN LILIUOKALANI

HUMPBACK WHALE

HAWAIIAN TRIGGERFISH

ALOHA STATE

YELLOW HIBISCUS

CANDLENUT

"THE LIFE OF THE LAND IS PERPETUATED IN RIGHTEOUSNESS"

DATE OF STATEHOOD

50. HAWAII August 21, 1959

Named for the Polynesian word *hawaiki*, meaning "homeland"

Honolulu

candlenut

Honolulu's Iolani Palace is the only royal residence in the U.S.

yellow hibiscus

nene

"JUSTICE FOR ALL"

SEAL OF THE PRESIDENT OF THE UNITED STATES

SCARLET OAK

WHITE HOUSE

WASHINGTON MONUMENT

WOOD THRUSH

CAPITOL

AMERICAN BEAUTY ROSE

LINCOLN MEMORIAL

WASHINGTON, D.C. July 16, 1790

Named in honor of George Washington and Christopher Columbus (District of Columbia)

The capital of the U.S.

scarlet oak

American Beauty rose

wood thrush

The Supreme Court has its own independent police force, which is responsible for a one-block area.

A note about the illustrations in this book

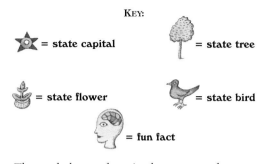

KEY:

= state capital

= state tree

= state flower

= state bird

= fun fact

The symbols, people, animals, scenes, and designs on each wagon are pictured for a reason. Look for the story behind each picture. Visit your library and the Internet and talk to your parents, relatives, teachers, and friends to learn more about the states. If you created your own train of states, what would you draw on each wagon? Here are some leads to get you started:

1. **DELAWARE:** Can you find a diamond on this wagon? Thomas Jefferson nicknamed Delaware "The Diamond State" in tribute to its small size but great strategic value.

2. **PENNSYLVANIA:** Binney & Smith invented Crayola Crayons in Easton in 1903. • Why is Benjamin Franklin pictured with a kite and key? • Did you know that Benjamin Franklin established the first library in the colonies?

3. **NEW JERSEY:** Can you spot George Washington? • Why are Aaron Burr and Alexander Hamilton dueling?

4. **GEORGIA:** The official state vegetable of Georgia is the sweet Vidalia onion. Can you find it here? • Georgia is the top producer of peanuts and peaches in the U.S.

5. **CONNECTICUT:** The Naval Submarine Base New London was the Navy's first submarine base.

6. **MASSACHUSETTS:** Can you spot Plymouth Rock? • The Boston Tea Party took place on December 16, 1773. • Who is standing to the left of the striped flag?

7. **MARYLAND:** King William's School opened in 1696. • The wild horses of Assateague Island are the size of ponies.

8. **SOUTH CAROLINA:** The "Best Friend of Charleston" (1830) was the first steam locomotive in the U.S. to offer a scheduled service for passengers.

9. **NEW HAMPSHIRE:** No two Concord Coaches were ever the same. Custom-painted and famous for comfort, these stagecoaches were built by the Abbot, Downing Company in Concord. Can you spot one here?

10. **VIRGINIA:** The Chesapeake Bay Bridge-Tunnel is 18 miles long and is the longest bridge-tunnel complex in the world. • The Virginia House of Delegate's Mace symbolizes the importance of government. Can you find it?

11. **NEW YORK:** Can you spot Niagara Falls? • Peter Sís, the author of this book, lives near Sunnyside, Washington Irving's home. Can you find two of Irving's creations here? • Fact or fiction: Peter Minuit bought Manhattan in 1626. • The last rivet on the Statue of Liberty was put into place in 1886.

12. **NORTH CAROLINA:** First flight! On December 17, 1903, the Wright brothers, Orville (right) and Wilbur, made three short flights at Kill Devil Hills, near Kitty Hawk. • Did you know that the first gold nugget in the U.S. was found in 1799 in Cabarrus County?

13. **RHODE ISLAND:** Newport was the site of the first circus in the U.S., in 1774. • Newport was founded in 1639 and was one of the busiest ports in the colonies.

14. **VERMONT:** Elisha Graves Otis, inventor of the elevator brake, was born near Halifax. Look for his name the next time you ride an elevator!

15. **KENTUCKY:** Abraham Lincoln and Jefferson Davis, key leaders of the Union and Confederacy, were born within nine months of each another and less than one hundred miles apart. Can you spot them here?

16. **TENNESSEE:** The Grand Ole Opry has been broadcasting live on the radio since 1925. Can you spot the musicians here? • Tennessee has more than 3,800 caves. • Davy Crockett was born August 17, 1786. His rifle was named "Old Betsy." • The state commercial fish is the channel catfish; the state game fish is the largemouth bass. What is the difference?

17. **OHIO:** Neil Armstrong was born August 5, 1930; John Glenn was born July 18, 1921. • The flying pigs on top of steamboat smokestacks guarding the entrance to Cincinnati's Bicentennial Commons recall a time when the city was nicknamed Porkopolis, a reference to the meat packing industry.

18. **LOUISIANA:** The St. Louis Cathedral was built in 1718. Can you find it? • The first Mardi Gras parade took place in New Orleans in 1857. • The Mississippi River reaches the Gulf of Mexico just south of New Orleans.

19. **INDIANA:** How long is the Indianapolis 500? • Indiana is one of the top five popcorn-producing states in the U.S. • On October 26, 1803, Meriwether Lewis and William Clark and the first members of the Corps of Discovery began their journey of exploration from the Falls of the Ohio, near Clarksville.

20. **MISSISSIPPI:** When President Theodore Roosevelt refused to shoot a bear cub near Onward, Morris Michtom stuffed a toy bear and called it "Teddy's Bear." • The slouch hat, originally a civilian hat, became part of the official uniform of the Confederate army during the Civil War.

21. **ILLINOIS:** Can you spot Ida B.Wells and Jane Addams? • The Sears Tower in Chicago was the tallest building in the world from 1973 to 1996.

22. **ALABAMA:** Why is cotton pictured here?

23. **MAINE:** August is Maine Lobster Month. • There are more than sixty lighthouses along Maine's coast.

24. **MISSOURI:** The Missouri River—"Big Muddy"—flows 2,315 miles before joining the Mississippi just north of St. Louis.

25. **ARKANSAS:** What is an Arkansan? • The nation's only active diamond mine is located near Murfreesboro.

26. **MICHIGAN:** Henry Ford and his son Edsel were both born in Michigan. • Pictured here is a 1916 Ford Model T.

27. **FLORIDA:** Florida has coastline on both the Atlantic Ocean and the Gulf of Mexico.

28. **TEXAS:** The battle of the Alamo took place in San Antonio, then called Bejar, in 1836. • The Lady Bird Johnson Wildflower Center is in Austin.

29. **IOWA:** The Red Delicious apple, originally grown near Peru by James (Jesse) Hiatt in the late 1800s, is one of the world's most popular varieties.

30. **WISCONSIN:** Magician Harry Houdini called Appleton his hometown, but he was really born in Budapest, Hungary.

31. **CALIFORNIA:** Gold was discovered at Sutter's Mill on January 24, 1848, and the California Gold Rush began.

32. **MINNESOTA:** Did you know that there are actually more than 15,000 lakes in the "Land of 10,000 Lakes?" • Sod houses, or "soddies," such as the one pictured here were made of layers of turf bricks. Could that be Laura Ingalls Wilder in the doorway?

33. **OREGON:** Mount Hood, a volcano in the Cascade Range, last erupted in 1805, just before the arrival of Lewis and Clark on October 18.

34. **KANSAS:** Amelia Earhart was born on July 24, 1897, in Atchison.

35. **WEST VIRGINIA:** Spruce Knob in the Appalachian Mountains is the highest point in the state. How high is it?

36. **NEVADA:** Camels were imported to Nevada in the 1850s and used as pack animals.

37. **NEBRASKA:** Nebraska is also called "The Tree Planter's State." • The state tree is the cottonwood; cottonwood trees were often landmarks for the pioneers.

38. **COLORADO:** The Great Sand Dunes National Monument & Preserve has dunes over 750 feet high.

39. **NORTH DAKOTA:** Black-tailed prairie dogs usually live in enormous "towns" covering one hundred or more acres.

40. **SOUTH DAKOTA:** Can you spot Sitting Bull and Crazy Horse? • Can you find Presidents Washington, Jefferson, Roosevelt, and Lincoln?

41. **MONTANA:** The Battle of the Little Bighorn (also known as Custer's Last Stand) was fought on June 25, 1876.

42. **WASHINGTON:** Can you spot Chief Seattle?

43. **IDAHO:** The russet Burbank (a potato introduced by Luther Burbank in 1872) is Idaho's most famous potato.

44. **WYOMING:** Wyoming is called the Equality State because it was the first state to give women the right to vote. Laramie's Louisa "Grandma" Swain cast the first ballot in 1870. • Is a bison the same thing as a buffalo?

45. **UTAH:** On May 10, 1869, lines constructed by the Central Pacific and Union Pacific Railroads were joined in Promontory by the Golden Spike, forming the first transcontinental railroad in the U.S.

46. **OKLAHOMA:** The Five Civilized Tribes were the Cherokee, Chickasaw, Choctaw, Creek, and Seminole.

47. **NEW MEXICO:** The Pueblo of Acoma is also known as Sky City because it's atop a 357-foot-tall mesa. • An international balloon festival takes place in Albuquerque every autumn.

48. **ARIZONA:** What do Gila monsters eat? • More than four million people visit the Grand Canyon National Park each year.

49. **ALASKA:** The Alaskan pipeline is 800 miles long. • How big is Alaska?

50. **HAWAII:** The Hawaiian Triggerfish is also called the humuhumunukunukuapua`a.

THE CABOOSE: WASHINGTON, D.C.: You can register to vote when you turn 18.